the flap pamphlet series

Modern Love

open, read, turn

Modern Love

the flap pamphlet series (No. 5)
Printed and Bound in the United Kingdom

Published by the flap series, 2011
the pamphlet series of flipped eye publishing
All Rights Reserved

Cover Design by Petraski
Series Design © flipped eye publishing, 2010

'I Walk The City At Night To Find You' appeared in Big Yeller
Magazine; 'Porthcothan Bay At Night' appeared in Scattered Reds
published by Bad Language Press; 'Wrapping Paper, 6" x 6"', and
'When A Thief Kisses You, Count Your Teeth' appeared in Cadaverine
Magazine; 'Vowel Speak' appeared in The Fib Review; 'Modern Love:
Texting' appeared in Popshot Magazine and 'Re: Memories' appeared
in Shot Glass Journal. I am grateful for the support of the Barbican
Centre's Young Poets Scheme where ( ), After, April Shower, Dandelion
Blows, Hiroshima Vow-Towers, Journeyman and Vowel Speak were
created.

ISBN-13: 978-1-905233-37-3

LOTTERY FUNDED

*For family, who we find as friends with time
and friends, the family of our own making.*

Modern Love

Max Wallis

Contents | *Modern Love*

September

Thinking Infinity

All the days to tread till I meet you. All the miles walking together around kitchens, homes and showrooms clutching our Tesco/Morrisons/Waitrose-trolley-full-dreams. Swearing whilst our kids watch us, getting in a huff over what type of juice is good. I'm young; I'm old, still thinking this. Every stolen pillow is a memory out of reach on a shelf with steam pressed showers, clammyfucked meek and sweet. On that ledge there's your bottom shaped in tea leaves, stained mugs and all the silent faceless dreams I've had. In nightcoiled alleys you're lamppost-flashing, winking a morse code language from a daylight, daybreak, future-never-seen and there at a place I can't reach you're dancing, smiling all-knowing because my feet can't walk through time yet. Try as they might I can't get the dance right. This could be five hundred poems, and it has and it will, every sky I'm under is over you, too; every time I sleep I'm eyetight, thinking of you clearly. All these drinks I've drowned, toasted dearly, dear. Every moment spent ticks towards our meeting, starbound, trapped, heavy heaving. Kissing. Like this. x. And this. x. And this. x.

October

Vowel Speak

Once,
I
met him
under a
vowel filled nighttime
of ohs, and yous, and ees, and Is.
Beneath the neon hued Can Club; just us, hands clenched tight
like crab claws. Mouths apart speaking of nothing, everything. The
    space between sighlences.

Ways Not To Fall In Love

I will not ask your name
in case it becomes my new lullaby
turned over and over again.

I will not kiss you first
in case, pecked, it remains with me
a silent signature of your lips.

I will not dance with you
in case the drink blurs your face into my dreams
watching between Love and Like.

I will not tell you my hopes
in case you fall for those
and not for me.

I will not speak to you
in case your voice begins to merge
with the heart-drum in my chest.

I will not text you quickly
or leave you kisses
in case I begin to fall and fall.

November

Journeyman

We took a journey.
After the drink

that somehow bridged our first hellos
then at night, as we attempted sleep,
the closed brackets of our bodies.

That night we carved new words in city stone,
bottomed glasses:
vodka and Diet Coke as our mouths,
judging, but kind,
spoke tomes
in the quiet move of *Zygomaticus major*
and minor
    and more.

First, of nervous probing,
a smirk as you laughed twice at my voice.
Then, gentle,
making motions that predicated words.

I focused on your lips.
The words unsounded through a kiss,
spoke against snowdrift streets.

Statues

We lie, two statues
scared,
scared of skin.

December

Modern Love: Texting

We send each other text messages at work.
Discuss what we're having for lunch.
Ether-joined by unlimited messages and pixel screens.
Two minutes after saying goodbye on dates
our phones jangle, vibrate,
'I had a lovely time tonight :-)'.

The little xx means more from you.
You give me fewer than my mum.
I look and linger at them, there,
at the end of your miniature letters.
Save the sweet ones in a folder
and read them when down.

'These are the reasons I love you.'
'Do you want to go to the cinema at four?'
'I've never felt this before.'
I smile when I see your name appear.

The lump is a plastic pebble in my pocket
heavy with the weight of expectancy.
Linked to everything, almost sentient
it throbs with the lives
of so many people a button press away:
Facebook, e-mails, Google
and you.

When people are gone: vanished.
Ephemeral ghosts that exist
but don't. That breathe,
but don't.
The wishing wells in which we shed our coins.
Our thumbs linger over 'DELETE'
as though they'll disappear from memory, too.

Punch. Gone. The love letter's dead.
Think that'll make us feel better.
When our hearts turn red again,
we'll wish we had the numbers still
to say
hello, hi, how do you do.

Wrapping Paper, 6" x 6"

In amongst all this packaging
I can feel you – the rip and tear of cardboard
and how you removed my clothes.

From the blue lines, the scrawled words,
I can trace your fingernibs
and unpluck your prints.

Touching the rough unstuck gum
I can kiss you
still.

All The Words

All the words forgotten,
words never said to strangers
on buses too shy to summon courage:
                    'Hi'.

All the words I've lost
in time, death, life,
bundled up in bodies not my own,
words I could have used and never will.

All the words I've played games with
   'love', 'forever', 'everything',
and been forgiven for playing.
'Sorry'.

The words I'm no longer afraid of,
      'I', 'us', 'we'.

Those I've found,
yours is the word that never dies
but burns and burns and burns.

January

( )

This pressing of bodies:
sticky palms from where we held the counterweight to ourself; then
    lips,
lending each other breath and broad trunked chests,
heavy with the silence of evening song.
You enfold the Matryoshka-doll-me.
We are a duet, playing the night game
in the forgotten worlds between owl-time and breakfast.
We murmur each other's names: dot-through-dot
and-dotted by the mmms of our notes.

A sharp clunk and my rattling head,
full of moths, fireflies and deadlines, wakes me.
Six-am dawn lays her fingers across the bones of your face.
Your feet, out, bare like dolphins against white linen waves.
I trip and fall.
You stir, grab and hold me into the nook,
the slotted jig, the saw of your neck; puck the air with your mouth.
I reach forwards, kiss, and curl up behind you
like a question mark of us.

February

When A Thief Kisses You, Count Your Teeth

Take my coat and hang it on the door. Rip my shirt,
button by popped button. Tie it around your waist.
Pick up little black things and put them in your pocket.
Undo my belt, wrench it until the loops split. Curl it.
Slide down skin-clung trousers. Fumble with my feet, my socks.
Cut off my boxers.

      Now, take in my scent and eyes.
Shave my hair, brows, pubes. Stuff them in a pillowcase.
Peel the dead skin from my heels. Tap my head
three times and unlock my skull. Open the cavity.
Prise out my brain and let it sit on the windowsill.
Shed my case and dump it by your bed. Wipe the blood
from my musculature and smear it on your clothes.

Dismember my limbs. Put my toes and fingers
in your dog's bowl. Crack open my ribs, suck the breath
from my lungs. Use my tendons as thread, my bones
as knitting needles. Gouge my eyes and add them
to the necklace you wear. Take it all. Everything. Now.

Morning

I'll leave the sheets as you desert them,
unmade, twisted.

Keep the last kiss you give me,
silent, rough with yearning.

Hold the darkness of night as we talk,
the blacks, whites of stars. Forever.

Won't eat to keep you in my mouth
or drink to have you there, in my throat.

I'll let the room remain still, not stagnant
but fostering. Growing.

Daylight would smash it all.

March

Little Things

An unwashed plate; we break two glasses half-emptied with wine and our Rioja stained mouths; time washes us in seconds that turn to days. Sunday, night; I sleep with my back turned to breath-sounds and the noise of silence. A hand curls around my hipbone; I shift away, a visitor in my quilts and the guilt of not-knowing-why. Head drums a beat of no, no, no. We do not make love. You try, and I insist. My mind is a curled up rosebud retreating. "There is nothing to be stressed about." Instead say: Why are you stressed? What's wrong? I'm sorry. It's okay. I love you.

Fairytale

Look through March rain veils
into sunscapes and green, green, woodland.
Take the pinch of reality and throw it behind you.
Do not let the other Megabus passengers see.
Swallow a Fisherman's Friend and travel.
Tannoys tinkle and it is three tomorrows
away and soaked in eucalyptus and tanging almost-pain.
Shudders turn to slipping lullabies
and windows open portal-wide
and now, breathe,
count to three … one … two …
and it is the turn for your eyes.
You have arrived.
Another man, dressed in imaginary nights
and dancing is waiting.
Hand him your lover's last words on his tongue
and with your other, take a strand of his fairy hair.
Hold him.
Do not let the world tug you back.
Focus.
Let him reach into his pocket and untuck a compact mirror
coated in the colour of heartache.
Open it.
Take back your smile.

April

Porthcothan Bay At Night

Here,
on wet grains,
the sea wipes sand
like rain across glass.
They sit under a tartan rug
hands down pants, fondling
as the fire cracks and chatter
spit-spurts between dark silhouettes
and ghoulish uplit faces.
They squeeze and pretend
that nothing is happening.

Tonight,
people leave, one by one,
and they remain alone
with the sea, gunblack,
which throws and turns,
a humongous tongue,
salivating.
They walk, hold hands
and kiss between rocks.
The water laps at their ankles;
stars stab white
in an upturned black basin.

Later,
as kisses turn from lips
to skin, to cloth and back,
the sea rushes forwards and retreats
a metronome to their throws.
Two sets of footsteps
stretch from rock to cove
where bent forwards,
arched back
they take turns.

After

Wake in the morning and weigh your heart
against hangover scales and remnant palms.

Do not wash to hold him against your skin
sigh and feel the weight of everything …

As another comes with blue-eyed guilt, bed
dressed in morning grubbery in your mind,

hear his nonsense sounds and taste, smell,
feel the reek of his five a.m. breath. Kiss

let the image shift, ripple, flex, awash again
with dew-dawn, on a cliff looking out at sea

as two bodies bring in the sun and sink
inside, retreat your hands behind your ribcage

with fear and text, text your other-love
with furious hands as though he can tell

through satellites and instant-time
what you have done. Give him extra kisses.

When he replies with just one,
give him none.

April Shower

A power cut, two half-baked smiles and the knowing silence of regret. Dark, dark as the grime soaked tray in your hands, charred peppers and too-fried onions. You are in the kitchen. Outside the world is a lacquered painting and running away. Water drips the pine tree across the pane and road. Drum. Drum. Drum-beats the glass. Inside the kettle stops its boiling midway and his face is covered in dropping tears. You are failing to make words form through a twisted out-of-batteries tongue. He closes his eyes and tries to hide his pain with what you have done. Wring your hands but still no verbs leap to lips. All you can presume is that there are no words left to say.

Leave the kitchen and slip into his bed fully clothed. Pretend to sleep. In the morning the rains and tears stop and dry you lie in bed broken by before. When the world shudders back to life and a sharp light switches on, your eyes turn with purple outlines of a haze. Groan. A few moments pass and in the kitchen hear the kettle begin again. He does not say a word. Relieve him of the silence. Creak. Leave before it boils.

A final glance. Sigh as the door slams a wooden tongue. Do not look back as dawn carries her torch across the sky; he will stay. Tarmac claps footsteps toward day and then, within, something out loud to the world that he will never hear; 'I am sorry, you know.'

May

Facebook

Modern love is not told in paper
but the pixels in a face trapped
and peering out, bound in comments,
tagged with us. Click, see friendship,
it is you and I, December, 'in a relationship',
flicking between pictures
from when we first met.
Forty-three people have liked
our solid-state love. Kiss kiss.
Heart heart. Smiley face.
Wink.

Facebook is like a photo album
for the mind and more forgetful.
It collects what we do not.
In March we shift to, 'it's complicated'.
(Acquaintances, not friends,
the people there to bolster numbers
and educate in networking, click
'like'.)
It always ends.

In time,
come May,

we are 'single'.
Facebook has updated but we are still
in this state;
you find three messages from a boy
that has been in my head for two months.
We end.

Spend our days stalking
clicking through the photos of each other
that now hold alien men where once
we were two halves of mussel shells.
A couple.
Now, separate
as salt dough to sweet.
We send niceties. Discuss politics. Say hello.
Someone finds an old disposable camera
from a trip to Blackpool Pleasure Beach,
they upload it and tag us,
kissing with rock between our mouths
like lady and the tramp, but trampier.

You can trace the history
of real life, of us, of ourness
through MySQL databases,
notes, see friendship, click,
like, click, love,
click, love. Click, account.
Log out.

Hiroshima Vow-Towers

1945: bomb-first dropped; American deterrence.
Day like today but the sun rose twice. Once,
spread soft in morning.
The other violent soon after,
white with mourning:
a man and his wife, the sheets tossed.
Him outside in underwear and watching
shadows play-writhing on grass.
A flash then black.
Two flesh loves surviving
where buildings ripple waved stone.
Birds puffed ash popping.
These two,
with glass in their necks and thighs,
walked wasteland silent, hands clasped.

2010's German heiress divorce battle-won
100 million pound fortune, done.
A post-break pre-nup check;
four years to prove the disconnect.
To vow to marry for love.

9/11, 2001: planes hit.
An England boy, me.
School to home to watch TV.
Cos he's young,

cartoon-cancelled annoyed.
Towers toppling instead.

With us I'm sure it was never love.
Atomic, forceful, yes, but there were no vows
in the kiss touch of two bodies pressing skin.
Two towers towering tall.
Mostly drunk, back-thinking, to how we were,
how we did not spend time but waste it.
Two birds, now,
black charred in ash in the wake
of breaking.

June

I Walk The City At Night To Find You.

I walk the city at night to find you.
Clockworked windup feet carry me
on buses, through alleys,
away from crowds.

Absent, I drift.
Night time's a clown
rubbing off its make-up.

Every face
yours:
    this is you sad
    this is you happy
    this is you black
    old
    straight.

I walk and walk and walk.
Buildings are trees.
There's no GPS or breadcrumbs
for a beating heart.

I sit by the wheel for ten minutes,
wait, watch,
then leave.

July

Re:Memories

These things embed
like YouTube clips
on loop.

In the head before sleep
under covers,
one-man shivering.

In libraries, shops,
cafeterias, at bus stops,
eyesight flitting out of reality;

clicking play, again
and again,
again.

August

Lonely Hearts United

Here,
in this city
right now
you are one of thousands.

In all these empty seats
where people sat and still the heat
travels through to me,
you are here, waiting.

The impressions of breath on glass
and the stroke of greasy hands
as they traced "I love you"
we could kiss and not know it.

In the prints on bus bells,
coat rails, glasses,
   we will have touched before
and for a moment held hands.

I write an advertisement and post it on Gumtree,
Facebook, and in Guardian Soulmates

"Lonely Hearts United
Platt Fields Park
Manchester
Saturday, three-pm.
Picnic."

It passes, people click 'maybe'.
On the day, I draw up in my car
and watch as the heartaching gather.
In cowardice I sit and watch
and do not meet.
Watching as couples form.

Social Love

Love is imaginary;
Laura is bitter and a spinster
will die alone surrounded by cats.
Liked by one person.
Renewal, indescribable, fuel.
Everything.
Beauty – painful – reunion: complicated.
Snug.
I meant to write smug but predictive text
got the better of me and now
I think it's right.
  Bollocks.
Essential.
Contentment.
Conversation and gratification – complicated.
Fickle. Trust. Commitment.
Laura, you say that like it's a bad thing. Hell,
that's my ambition but it keeps going wrong.
Renewal. And opening.
Absolution, inspiration.
Gut-wrench feat. ecstasy.
A word –
which finds its meaning in its use within a larger
complex chain. Searching for the meta
physical beneath language is pointless.
You should know that.
Sacrificial – everything.

Love is patient. Kind. Does not envy, does not boast.
Is not proud nor rude or self-seeking.
Doesn't keep a record of wrongs, nor
delights in evil but rejoices with
the truth. It always protects, always
perseveres and never fails.
I knew I was doing something wrong.
In b4 pr0n.
Divorce is better.
Acceptance xx.

On January 6th 2011 I asked people on Facebook to respond to what love means to them – in one word. Naturally, people being people and not prone to following instructions they ended up having conversations and including sentences.

Dandelion Blows

In a field in summer, gin-drenched with grief
I close eyes and fumble words.

A dandelion:
thinks of me,
thinks me not,
of St James' Passage where our lips
found the underside of cotton briefs,
places we still live in memory-touch,

The sun slides her wings against me,
barley ticks and tocks its metronome
rustling in the cliff-winds of Cornwall
and Porthcothan Bay.

and all the hours now nothing meant
and try,

I trace my skin
down the accordion of my ribcage
fumbling with the keys you pressed and
there, between my navel and my chest
where you lay your head.

and try,
I know that part of you knows, that part
that looks at your phone just as it rings
the one whose doors open
just as he leans to the handle,

The sea is making his throat churns,
sea spray spits across closed eyes.
My stomach is turning.

                                        is feeling now.
              If I walk where we walked, drink what we drank,
        if I sit and make hot chocolates with real melted chocolate
                    just like we did on our thirsty dates.
              Close my eyes wish and wish till dawn comes
                        turns to dusk and try,

If I think hard enough
you'll know.
                                    you'll know.

Allow yourself this one day

hungover from love. To sit in your sad cocoon
bed-lain on lemon bon bon sheets and sick with ache,
cuddling your bones. Let the day roll into night.
Do not fret about the red numbers in your account,
about deadlines and business worries; pick up three
books and do not read them. Wallow in coffee,
or simply nothing, as you tap-tap through Twitter feeds
and text messages and nonsense mad thoughts.
Let yourself reek with the unwash of sleep-sweats
and salt tears. Eat the mirror on your wall.
Play the unhappy songs that in bed you kissed,
had sex, made love to, that time, when sex became
heart-bare: skintouched, and *those* eyes.

Tomorrow you can sit in the warmth of a bath
clean your nails, pluck your brow, shave the fluff;
eat, drink, clean your room of your last meals
and bed-locked naked picnics. Tomorrow you can sail
in fresh linen and clothes, listen to happy songs
with no meaning but pop-tones, through a new day;
today is today, this day, my love.

Lightning Source UK Ltd.
Milton Keynes UK
UKOW04f0647180316

270443UK00004B/67/P